ST. ANDREW

CHRISTMAS

NOVENA

PRAYER

BOOK

CONTENT

INTRODUCTION

The St. Andrew Christmas Novena, also known as the Christmas expectation Prayer, is a beautiful and traditional devotion observed by numerous Christians as they prepare their hearts for the joyful festivity of the birth of Jesus Christ. This novena is named after Saint Andrew the Apostle, whose feast day falls on November 30th, and it traditionally begins on that date.

During this special time of prayer and reflection, religionists turn their hearts towards the significance of the Nativity, planning on the profound mystifications girding the birth of our Savior. The novena consists of a sequence of nine prayers, each with its own unique reflection, which are recited daily in the days leading up to Christmas.

In this companion, we will explore the history and meaning of theSt. Andrew Christmas Novena, offer practical advice on how to prepare for and engage in this spiritual practice, and give diurnal reflections and prayers for each of the nine days. Whether you're new to this tradition or a seasoned party, may this companion enrich your spiritual trip during this blessed season of stopgap, love, and expectation. Let us embark together on this meaningful trip of prayer and contemplation as we prepare to drink the Christ Child into our hearts and homes.

1

THE HISTORY AND SIGNIFICANCE OF ST. ANDREW'S FEAST DAY

Andrew's Feast Day, celebrated on November 30th, holds a significant place in Christian tradition and is nearly associated with the St. Andrew Christmas Novena. Then, we claw into the history and significance of this special day

literal Background

The Apostle Andrew St. Andrew, also known as Andrew the Apostle, was one of the twelve apostles chosen by Jesus Christ during his fleshly ministry. He was the family of St. Peter and played a vital part in the early spread of Christianity.

Significance of St. Andrew's Feast Day

2. Patron Saint of Scotland St. Andrew is the patron saint of Scotland, and his feast day is a public vacation in Scotland.

The St. Andrew's Cross, a white saltire on a blue field, is a prominent symbol of Scotland and appears on its flag.

Connection to the St. Andrew Christmas Novena The choice of November 30th as the starting date for the St. Andrew Christmas Novena is significant. It marks the morning of the liturgical season of Advent, a time of medication and expectation for the birth of Jesus. St. Andrew's feast day serves as a befitting starting point for this period of spiritual reflection.

Martyrdom St. Andrew is believed to have been martyred by crucifixion on anX-shaped cross(known as a saltire). This unique form of martyrdom further emphasizes his association with the cross and Christ's immolation.

Global Observance St. Andrew's Feast Day isn't only celebrated in Scotland but also honored in numerous other corridor of the world. It serves as a day for Christians to recognize the memory and benefactions of this backer.

As we embark on the St. Andrew Christmas Novena, it's essential to understand the literal and spiritual significance of St. Andrew's Feast Day. This day marks the morning of a season of spiritual medication and reflection, inviting us to follow in the steps of this devoted backer as we await the birth of the Savior.

How to pray the novena

Step 1: Prepare Your Space
Choose a quiet and comfortable place for prayer. You may want to light a candle or create a peaceful atmosphere to help you focus.

Step 2: Begin on November 30th
Traditionally, the novena starts on November 30th, the feast day of St. Andrew. However, you can begin it later if needed.

Step 3: Daily Recitation
Each day, from November 30th until Christmas Eve, recite the St. Andrew Christmas Novena prayer 15 times. Some people prefer to break this into three sets of five recitations each.

Step 4: Reflect on the Meaning
After reciting the prayer, take a moment to reflect on the meaning of the words and the anticipation of Christ's birth. Consider your intentions, hopes, and desires for the Christmas season.

Step 5: Personal Intentions
On the ninth and final day of the novena, after reciting the prayer and reflection, add your personal intentions. These can be prayers for yourself, loved ones, or broader concerns.

Step 6: Conclude with a Closing Prayer

End each day with a closing prayer, such as the Our Father or a heartfelt expression of gratitude for the opportunity to prepare for the birth of Jesus.

Step 7: Continue Your Advent Journey

As you pray the St. Andrew Christmas Novena, remember that it's a special way to deepen your spiritual connection during Advent. Embrace the sense of anticipation and hope as you approach Christmas.

Step 8: Celebrate Christmas

On Christmas Day, rejoice in the birth of Jesus Christ, reflecting on the spiritual preparation and devotion of the novena that led you to this joyful moment.

By following these steps, you can pray the St. Andrew Christmas Novena and experience the profound sense of spiritual preparation and anticipation that it brings during the Advent season.

NOVENA PRAYERS

DAY 1
THE FIRST PRAYER OF THE NOVENA

Reflection

As we begin this St. Andrew Christmas Novena, we flash back the moment when the Son of God, Jesus Christ, was born of the Virgin Mary in Bethlehem. This humble and miraculous event marked the morning of God's extraordinary plan for our deliverance. In the midst of the piercing cold wave of that night hour, the light of the world came into being. Let us reflect on the wonder and significance of Christ's birth as we embark on this trip of prayer and medication for the Christmas season.

Prayer

" Hail and blessed be the hour and moment in which the Son of God was born of the most pure Abecedarian Mary, at night, in Bethlehem, in the piercing cold wave. In that hour, vouchsafe, O my God! to hear my prayer and grant my solicitations through the graces of Our Savior Jesus Christ, and of His Blessed mama. Amen."

Take a moment to recite this prayer and reflect on the profound meaning of Christ's birth in your own life. May this novena consolidate your connection to the phenomenon of Christmas and fill your heart with stopgap and joy.

DAY 2
THE ALTERNATE PRAYER OF THE NOVENA

Reflection

On this alternate day of the St. Andrew Christmas Novena, we continue our trip of expectation. moment, we reflect on the riddle of the manifestation, where the Word came meat and dwelt among us. God's bottomless love for humanity is revealed in this profound moment. As we meditate on the manifestation, let us open our hearts to the transformative power of Christ's presence in our lives.

Prayer

" Hail and blessed be the hour and moment in which the Son of God was born of the most pure Abecedarian Mary, at night, in Bethlehem, in the piercing cold wave. In that hour, vouchsafe, O my God! to hear my prayer and grant my solicitations through the graces of Our Savior Jesus Christ, and of His Blessed mama. Amen."

Recite this prayer, and as you do, contemplate the extraordinary act of God taking on mortal form. How does the manifestation inspire you to draw near to Christ during this Advent season? May your reflection consolidate your faith andfill you with gratefulness for God's loving presence in your life.

DAY 3
THE THIRD PRAYER OF THE NOVENA

Reflection

On this third day of the St. Andrew Christmas Novena, we consider the significance of the Divine Word. In the morning, the Word was with God, and the Word was God. Through this Word, all effects were created, and in this Word, we find life and light. As we reflect on the Divine Word, let us seek to open our hearts to admit the Word made meat, Jesus Christ, and allow His verity to guide our lives.

Prayer

" Hail and blessed be the hour and moment in which the Son of God was born of the most pure Abecedarian Mary, at night, in Bethlehem, in the piercing cold wave. In that hour, vouchsafe, O my God! to hear my prayer and grant my solicitations through the graces of Our Savior Jesus Christ, and of His Blessed mama. Amen."

Recite this prayer, and contemplate the profound riddle of the Word getting incarnate in Jesus Christ. How does this verity shape your understanding of God's presence in the world? May this reflection consolidate your connection to the Word of God and inspire you to live in His light.

DAY 4
THE FOURTH PRAYER OF THE NOVENA

Reflection

As we continue our trip through the St. Andrew Christmas Novena, we reflect on the gift of grace. God's grace is the unmerited favor and love that He bestows upon us. It's through God's grace that we find remission, redemption, and the pledge of eternal life. During this Advent season, let us contemplate the immense gift of grace that came into the world with the birth of Jesus Christ.

Prayer

" Hail and blessed be the hour and moment in which the Son of God was born of the most pure Abecedarian Mary, at night, in Bethlehem, in the piercing cold wave. In that hour, vouchsafe, O my God! to hear my prayer and grant my solicitations through the graces of Our Savior Jesus Christ, and of His Blessed mama. Amen."

Recite this prayer, and reflect on the grace that Christ's birth brings to humanity. How has God's grace touched your life, and how can you extend grace and love to others during this season of Advent? May your contemplation lead to a deeper appreciation of the gift of God's grace.

DAY 5
THE FIFTH PRAYER OF THE NOVENA

Reflection

On this fifth day of the St. Andrew Christmas Novena, we turn our hearts toward Mary, the most pure Abecedarian and the mama of Jesus. Mary played a vital part in God's plan for deliverance, and her" yes" to God's will is an illustration of faith and obedience. As we reflect on Mary's part in the Nativity, let us seek her supplication and strive to emulate her devotion to God's plan.

Prayer

" Hail and blessed be the hour and moment in which the Son of God was born of the most pure Abecedarian Mary, at night, in Bethlehem, in the piercing cold wave. In that hour, vouchsafe, O my God! to hear my prayer and grant my solicitations through the graces of Our Savior Jesus Christ, and of His Blessed mama. Amen."

Recite this prayer, and contemplate the profound part that Mary played in the birth of Jesus. How can you model her faith and rendition to God's will in your own life? May your reflection consolidate your connection to Mary as a source of alleviation and guidance during this Advent season.

DAY 6
THE SIXTH PRAYER OF THE NOVENA

Reflection

On this sixth day of the St. Andrew Christmas Novena, we turn our attention to St. Joseph, the fleshly father of Jesus. Joseph played a pivotal part in the Nativity story, furnishing protection and guidance for Mary and the Christ Child. His quiet and biddable spirit serves as an illustration of trust in God's plan. As we reflect on Joseph's part in the Nativity, let us seek his supplication and strive to emulate his fastness and devotion.

Prayer

" Hail and blessed be the hour and moment in which the Son of God was born of the most pure Abecedarian Mary, at night, in Bethlehem, in the piercing cold wave. In that hour, vouchsafe, O my God! to hear my prayer and grant my solicitations through the graces of Our Savior Jesus Christ, and of His Blessed mama. Amen."

Recite this prayer, and contemplate the significance of St. Joseph's presence in the Holy Family. How can you draw alleviation from his trust in God's plan and his part as a protection and provider? May your reflection consolidate your connection toSt. Joseph and his illustration of faith during this Advent season.

DAY 7
THE SEVENTH PRAYER OF THE NOVENA

Reflection

On this seventh day of the St. Andrew Christmas Novena, we reflect on the goatherds' adoration of the invigorated Christ. The goatherds, humble and simple, were the first to admit the news of Jesus' birth from the angels. They responded with admiration and faith, speeding to Bethlehem to worship the Savior. As we meditate on their adoration, let us seek to approach Jesus with the same modesty, wonder, and reverence.

Prayer

" Hail and blessed be the hour and moment in which the Son of God was born of the most pure Abecedarian Mary, at night, in Bethlehem, in the piercing cold wave. In that hour, vouchsafe, O my God! to hear my prayer and grant my solicitations through the graces of Our Savior Jesus Christ, and of His Blessed mama. Amen."

Recite this prayer, and contemplate the goatherds' simple yet profound response to the communication of Christ's birth. How can you cultivate a heart of modesty and wonder in your own approach to the Savior? May your reflection consolidate your adoration and devotion to the invigorated King during this Advent season.

DAY 8
THE EIGHTH PRAYER OF THE NOVENA

Reflection

On this eighth day of the St. Andrew Christmas Novena, we turn our studies to the Magi, the Wise Men from the East, who followed the star to find the invigorated King. These trippers embarked on a trip of faith and discovery, offering precious gifts to recognize the Christ Child. As we reflect on the Magi's trip, let us consider our own trip of faith and the gifts we bring to offer to Jesus.

Prayer

" Hail and blessed be the hour and moment in which the Son of God was born of the most pure Abecedarian Mary, at night, in Bethlehem, in the piercing cold wave. In that hour, vouchsafe, O my God! to hear my prayer and grant my solicitations through the graces of Our Savior Jesus Christ, and of His Blessed mama. Amen."

Recite this prayer, and contemplate the trip and gifts of the Magi. How can you follow the light of Christ in your life's trip, and what gifts can you offer to recognize Him? May your reflection consolidate your commitment to seek and worship the Savior during this Advent season.

DAY 9
THE NINTH PRAYER OF THE NOVENA

Reflection

On this ninth and final day of the St. Andrew Christmas Novena, we turn our hearts to our particular intentions and solicitations. Just as we've reflected on colorful aspects of the Nativity story and drawn alleviation from the characters and events, now is the time to offer our own expedients, dreams, and needs to the Lord. As we conclude this novena, let us present our intentions with faith and trust, knowing that God hears our prayers.

Prayer

" Hail and blessed be the hour and moment in which the Son of God was born of the most pure Abecedarian Mary, at night, in Bethlehem, in the piercing cold wave. In that hour, vouchsafe, O my God! to hear my prayer and grant my solicitations through the graces of Our Savior Jesus Christ, and of His Blessed mama. Amen."

Recite this prayer, and take a moment to offer your particular intentions to God. What expedients and solicitations do you carry in your heart as you approach Christmas? Trust that God hears and knows the solicitations of your heart and will respond according to His God's will.

As we conclude this novena, may your faith be strengthened, and may you witness the presence and blessings of Christ in your life during this sacred season of Christmas.

CONCLUSION

As we conclude this St. Andrew Christmas Novena companion, we reflect on the trip we have accepted together in medication for the festivity of the birth of Jesus Christ. This nine- day devotion has allowed us to immerse ourselves in the beauty and significance of the Nativity story, drawing alleviation from crucial moments and numbers.

Throughout this novena, we've contemplated the birth of Christ in Bethlehem, the part of St. Andrew, the patronage of St. Joseph and Mary, the humble adoration of the goatherds, and the wisdom of the Magi. We have also offered our particular intentions and solicitations to the Lord, trusting in His grace and providence.

As we step down from this novena, may the spirit of expectation, stopgap, and joy remain with us. Let the assignments and reflections from this trip guide us in living out the true meaning of Christmas — drinking the Christ Child into our hearts and participating His love, peace, and goodwill with the world.

May this Christmas season be a time of renewal, heightening our faith, and drawing us near to the source of all light and love. Let us carry the communication of the Christ Child's birth with us, not only during this season but throughout the time, as a memorial of the profound gift of deliverance.

Thank you for embarking on this spiritual trip with us. May your Christmas be filled with blessings, and may the love of Christ shine brightly in your life and the lives of those you encounter. Merry Christmas and a blessed New Year!

You can write down your wish here

Made in United States
Orlando, FL
01 December 2024

54743534R00017